# The Mystery Seeds

**by Myka-Lynne Sokoloff**
**illustrated by Gabriele Antonini**

Uncle Hank has a garden.
I want a garden, too.

Uncle Hank said, "I have
seeds in the shed."

We found the seeds. They are mystery seeds.

"What will grow?" I asked.

I planted my mystery seeds.
Uncle Hank gave them water.
Then we waited for them
to grow.

I helped pull weeds.

Uncle Hank said, "We don't want weeds to grow here."

It got sunny, and my
plants grew.
The stems got taller.
The leaves got bigger.

My plants grew and grew.
Look at my mystery
seeds now!

Now we have food to eat.
We have seeds for our next
garden, too!